For Thales Moir Rowe — ALB

For my sister — we are two aspen trees sharing
roots, hearts, lives … & snacks — CS

Text copyright © 2024 by Annette LeBox
Illustrations copyright © 2024 by Crystal Smith

The publisher would like to thank Dr. Allen Larocque, forest ecologist, forester and data analyst, for checking the text and illustrations. Any error that may have crept in along the way is our own.

Published in 2024 by Groundwood Books / House of Anansi Press
groundwoodbooks.com

We gratefully acknowledge for their financial support of our publishing program the Canada Council for the Arts, the Ontario Arts Council and the Government of Canada.

Canada Council   Conseil des Arts
for the Arts   du Canada

ONTARIO ARTS COUNCIL
CONSEIL DES ARTS DE L'ONTARIO
an Ontario government agency
un organisme du gouvernement de l'Ontario

With the participation of the Government of Canada
Avec la participation du gouvernement du Canada | Canada

Library and Archives Canada Cataloguing in Publication
Title: Mother aspen / words by Annette LeBox ; pictures by Crystal Smith.
Names: LeBox, Annette, author. | Smith, Crystal (Artist)
Description: "A story of how forests cooperate and communicate."
Identifiers: Canadiana (print) 20230587763 | Canadiana (ebook) 20230587771 | ISBN 9781773069357 (hardcover) | ISBN 9781773069364 (Kindle) | ISBN 9781773069371 (EPUB)
Subjects: LCSH: Forest ecology—Juvenile literature. | LCSH: Aspen—Juvenile literature. | LCSH: Mycorrhizal fungi—Juvenile literature. | LCSH: Forest conservation—Juvenile literature. | LCGFT: Informational works. | LCGFT: Picture books.
Classification: LCC QH541.5.F6 L43 2024 | DDC j577.3—dc23

The illustrations were created with digital paint and layered textures.
Edited by Emma Sakamoto
Designed by Michael Solomon and Lucia Kim
Printed and bound in China

MIX
Paper | Supporting
responsible forestry
FSC
www.fsc.org   FSC® C144853

MOTHER ASPEN

WORDS BY

Annette LeBox

PICTURES BY

Crystal Smith

GROUNDWOOD BOOKS
HOUSE OF ANANSI PRESS
TORONTO / BERKELEY

In early spring, the Mother Tree wakens.
Her name is Quaking Aspen.
When the wind sings, she dances,
    branches reaching to the sun.

As the earth warms, she sends up sprouts
    from her roots.
The sprouts are her children. They look like
    many separate trees,
but they are a single tree, a mighty Mother
    Tree, hundreds of years old.

Perching on a hollow stump, a ruffed grouse performs a drum solo. He pumps his wings, a low sonic boom, to attract a mate.

At dusk, a moose and her calf browse on Aspen's bark.

In the sunlight, Aspen's leaves produce sugar.
Trees use sugar to grow wood and bark and leaves.
Like human children, young trees love sweets!

Beneath the earth, fungi wrap soft cottony threads around Aspen's roots.
Fungi can't produce sugar, so the Mother Tree feeds them too.

In exchange, fungi carry underground messages from tree to tree.
The messages warn the trees of drought, disease or insect infestations.

Aspen and spruce, fir and pine
have lively conversations!

As the temperature rises, Aspen catkins burst
    into bloom.
The catkin fruits crack open to release millions of
    tiny cotton-like seeds.

Wind blankets the ground with a delicate white fluff.
A flock of jays fill their bellies.

Sometimes an animal or bird buries a seed,
so next year a baby aspen might sprout.

By late spring, Mother Aspen has unfurled all of her leaves.
The slightest breeze sets them aflutter,
then her lullaby begins — a soft shush-shush-shushing.

A fox and her kits emerge from their underground den.
The three look up, ears pricked, listening to the trees sing.

As the sun grows warmer, Aspen leaves produce more sugar.
Sugar provides her with energy to grow.
Her canopy widens. Her trunk thickens.
Wildflowers sprout in the bunchgrass below.

Summer is a time of plenty
    in the Aspen grove.
Bears grow fat on berries and grasses.
Owls feed their hatchlings mice and voles.

When the Aspens grow thirsty
    in the summer heat,
fungi release their water reserves
    to feed them.
Like best friends, trees and fungi help
    each other survive.

By late summer, Mother Aspen's sugar-factory slows.
Sugar flows from her canopy to her trunk.
When the nights grow colder, her leaves turn golden.

In the autumn, birds gather to migrate.
Bats hibernate in tree cavities.

Fungi produce fruiting bodies called mushrooms.
The mushrooms sprout in the forest understory.

At the first hint of frost, Mother Aspen drops her leaves.
The leaves form a warm blanket around the saplings.

Soon snow dresses the Aspen grove in white.
A raven's cry breaks the quiet.
Mother Aspen and her young sleep until spring.

Weeks turn into years.
Centuries pass, yet Mother Aspen still stands,
sharing and caring for her community.

Until one morning, storm clouds gather.
Raindrops patter on the old tree's leaves.
Water runs from her canopy to her roots,
loosening the earth beneath the tree.

Lightning flashes!
Thunder booms!
Wind shakes the Mother Tree's crown.
It whips her branches and bends her trunk
until her heartwood shatters and the old tree
slowly falls to the ground, limbs broken,
sap flowing into her open wound.

As the Mother Tree takes her last breath,
she passes on her wisdom to the next generation.

Fungi spread the news through her vast underground threads.
Our mother is dead.

In time, Mother Aspen will become a nurse log.
She'll feed her seedlings sweets as her heartwood breaks down.

She'll dream of her young trees, how they'll grow straight
and strong, how they'll reach for the sky to face the sun,
how one sapling may grow taller than the others.

And in years to come, she may become a mighty Mother Tree.